KAIZEN FOREVER

Teachings of Chihiro Nakao

Kaizen for the Next Generation

Bob Emiliani
Katsusaburo Yoshino
Rudy Go

Kaizen Forever: Teachings of Chihiro Nakao / M.L. "Bob" Emiliani, Katsusaburo Yoshino, Rudy Go

Cover illustration by Chihiro Nakao. Used with permission. Other illustrations by Nakao-san or Shingijutsu USA used with permission. Cover design by Bob Emiliani.

Photographs by Bob Emiliani and Katsusaburo Yoshino.

ISBN-13: 978-0-9898631-0-0

Library of Congress Control Number: 2015905810

1. Organizational improvement 2. Kaizen 3. Lean management 4. Leadership 5. Business 6. Economics

First Edition: June 2015

Published by The CLBM, LLC, Wethersfield, Connecticut, USA

Manufactured using digital print-on-demand technology.

Chihiro Nakao leading Shingijutsu-kaizen.

Nakao-san

Thank you for your kindness and generosity.

Shingijutsu-Kaizen

Illustration by Chihiro Nakao

"Nobody will know kaizen without seeing it and nothing will be accomplished without doing it!!"

- Chihiro Nakao, F.O.M.

CONTENTS

Preface

Kaizen Forever introduces you to the teachings of Chihiro Nakao. Mr. Nakao (hereafter, Nakao-san, to show respect) co-founded the Shingijutsu Company in 1987 at the behest of Taiichi Ohno to teach the principles and practices of the Toyota Production System to a wider audience. The method for doing this is "learn by doing." The Japanese word "shingijutsu" literally means "new technology," as in new *management* technology. But, the word "shingijutsu" has deeper meaning, which you will learn about in Chapter 1.

Prior to founding Shingijutsu, Nakao-san worked for 27 years for Toyota Group. During that time he was mentored and trained by Mr. Ohno, who is recognized as the father of the Toyota Production System. Nakao-san is one of just a handful of people to have had that experience.

Nakao-san has long been the guardian of Shingijutsu's kaizen art and practices, and as such has worked tirelessly to preserve and expand the teachings of Mr. Ohno. We, along with many others, have been beneficiaries of that difficult and dedicated effort.

Nakao-san's teachings have enlightened us on wide-ranging subjects related to business, management, leadership, and more. He has done this in ways that nobody else has, and as no one else alive can. He has made a deep impact on us in practical, intellectual, and emotional ways. We want to share that with you.

Nakao-san has taught us far more than just production systems for manufacturing businesses. He has taught about things that apply to any business. Most people focus on the tools and therefore see only what is visible on the surface. He challenged us to think and see high above and deep below the surface, to see the whole picture in three dimensions. He challenged us to be brave explorers rather than timid conformists.

There are limitations to how many people Nakao-san can personally touch with his teachings. And, people often unconsciously limit what they are willing to learn as a result of prior experiences. Because of this, we undertook the challenge to write about his teachings and share with you some of the things that he has taught us.

We hope to express in these pages a sense of Nakao-san's perspective, how he thinks, his philosophy of kaizen, his enthusiasm for kaizen, his views on the socio-economic activity known as "business," and what we have learned from him.

We also hope to convey the view that competition in business must have the positive effect of strengthening people, and that kaizen builds human capability in response to competitive challenges. In contrast, mindless cutting in response to competition weakens people and weakens the ability of a business to compete.

Make no mistake, Nakao-san is the master and we are his pupils. We are still learning. That means, we continue to learn from things we learned in the past, we are learning in the present, and we think deeply about learning for the future.

Therefore, the best we can do is present to you an approximation of his teachings and of our learnings at the time of this writing. The moment this book was published, we learned new things that we cannot so easily tell you about. But, do not feel left behind. Instead, be brave and go forward on your own.

We also hope that this book inspires you in ways that closely match how we were inspired to think differently, to be practical and take action, and to learn and improve. Finally, we welcome your feedback.

Bob Emiliani
Wethersfield, Connecticut

Katsusaburo Yoshino
Saitama, Japan

Rudy Go
Bristol, Connecticut
28 May 2015

Kaizen For Future Generations

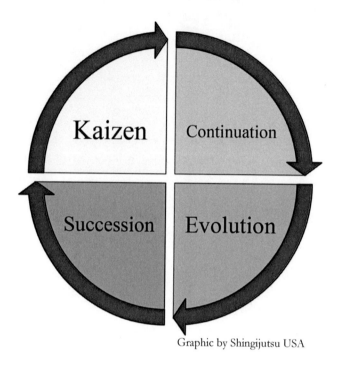

Graphic by Shingijutsu USA

Passing kaizen down to future generations to develop human thinking and capability for cost reduction. Please note the definition of "cost" can depend upon the responsibilities one has in an organization and the business process. Yet in all cases, costs internal or external to an organization can be reduced by kaizen.

Introduction

We wrote *Kaizen Forever* for anyone who wants to learn how to think or think better, made possible through "learn by doing." It will be of great interest to those who are curious and who are motivated and committed to kaizen. It will be of little interest to those who think they know how to think or those who are overconfident. An open mind captures useful knowledge that washes over closed minds.

Kaizen Forever does not teach Toyota's production system. Instead, we share the thinking that created Toyota's production system, whose principles and methods apply to any process in any kind of business or organization in any industry. In addition, we want readers to learn about business through the lens of kaizen. Through that lens, you will begin to see that the way you do work is, as Nakao-san would say, "No good."

However, it is not simply the fact that the way you do your work is "no good." Nakao-san taught us to think and expanded our understanding of what it means when the way we do our work is "no good:"

- How does it affect costs?
- How does it affect workers, managers, and the company?
- How does it affect customers, suppliers, investors, competitors, and society?
- What are the different socio-economic ways in which it impacts them?

- Negative impacts are bad for both people and for business and should be avoided. But how?

Historically, secondary and post-secondary teachers do not teach students the difference between batch-and-queue processing and flow. Batch-and-queue is better understood as "batch-and-non-flow," "non-flow," "flow-less," or "stagnant" processing. Batches are one of the results of non-flow.

Even today, batch-and-queue processing and flow are not recognized as fundamental and distinctive management practices used by organizations to process "material and information." It is important to note that, while we present material-and-information as two things, they are actually the same thing and are not separable (and therefore shown as hyphenated).

These are important differences that people should know about, preferably early in their careers rather than late. Why? Because anyone destined to work in an organization will surely encounter management based on batch-and-queue (stagnant) processing, and therefore have to contend with abnormalities related to cost, quality, lead-times, and dysfunctional organizational behaviors associated with it. When Nakao-san says, "That's no good," he is referring to batch-and-queue (stagnant) processing and the seven wastes, including the beliefs, behaviors, competencies, decision-making, practices, customs, and infrastructure that support it.

In contrast, flow is the lowest operating expense (and lowest total expense), highest quality, shortest lead-time way to process material-and-information. Kaizen is the means to achieve the seven flows: people, material (raw, parts, finished goods), equipment, information, and engineering. Yet, most organizations process material-and-information batch-and-queue, filled with the seven wastes. Why is that? And what can be done to improve?

Our dream is to reach younger generations, to inspire them to learn and practice kaizen and achieve flow. The generations that follow us want to make a difference. They want their lives to have more meaning and achieve higher levels of fulfillment at work and in life. *Kaizen Forever* will help show them how.

We also want to reach mid- and late-career managers who may be striving for greater meaning and fulfillment in their work as well. Our introduction to the teachings of Chihiro Nakao will help leaders recognize that their well-intentioned efforts have fallen far short of what is actually possible. Therefore, leaders must engage in learning new things. Nobody is exempt from improvement.

There are three items we would like you to take careful note of:

1) At no time do we talk about theory or ideal circumstances. The entirety of this book is grounded in the practical realm of the workplace.
2) *Kaizen Forever* is about kaizen, not specifically about manufacturing. Anything we say that derives from manufacturing also applies to service businesses.
3) There are no limitations to where kaizen can be applied. Any type of business or organization in any industry can benefit from kaizen.

Kaizen Forever does not provide answers to every question or offer clear direction for you to take. That is because your circumstances, while largely common with many other people and organizations, contain unique features. Whether common or unique, you need to think for yourself and you need to think forever. If we provide answers, then you will deceive yourself into thinking you know things that you do not know. You will not learn. Therefore, we want to put you into positions where you have to think, perhaps for long periods of time, so that the learning is all yours.

- Why is batch-and-queue (stagnant processing) perfectly suited for sellers' markets?
- Why is flow perfectly suited for buyers' markets?

To that end, *Kaizen Forever* is not intended to be read once and then put aside. It should be read again and again. Each time you read this book, we believe you will gain new, practical insights that will inspire you to take action.

As Nakao-san teaches:

"Kaizen means taking action; go to the genba now, deal with the facts now. Always take action; that is the key."

There is no end to kaizen. There is no end to what you can learn from this book.

Finally, please keep in mind that kaizen is the means for achieving Shingijutsu's production method, called "Shingijutsu Production SiQmi." The purpose of Shingijutsu Production SiQmi is to reduce costs, while the primary goal is improving productivity by focusing on non-cost measures such as time, quantity, distance, etc. In addition, quantity control, quality assurance, and respect for humanity are goals that must be achieved simultaneously and that support cost reduction through productivity improvement by various means. Kaizen, must therefore contribute to achieving the purpose and goals.

It is critically important to recognize that in Shingijutsu-kaizen, cost reduction is understood to result in simultaneous improvement in all parameters such as productivity, quality, lead-time, customer satisfaction, market share respect for humanity, profits, and so on. Shingijutsu-kaizen does not make trade-offs, where one parameter is made better and another parameter is made worse. It does not make sense to reduce costs and simultaneously introduce trade-offs that have negative effects on employees, suppliers, customers, investors, or communities.

We also want to make clear the importance of the words used to guide improvement. Language must be precise so that its real meaning is clear and vividly expresses the context. Nakao-san teaches never to use the word "problem" or "issue" because these words generalize and cover up the real meaning.

Use the word "abnormality" instead, which refers to a normal (standard) condition. This must be clearly defined and written on a sheet of paper for each operator, putting all necessary information of quality check, safety precautions, standard work-in-process, takt time, and cycle time. This enables everybody to easily identify either normal or abnormal against standards. Details such as these make a large difference with respect to kaizen results.

1

Shingijutsu Production SiQmi

Before we discuss Shingijutsu-kaizen, it is important for readers to first understand what the name of the company, Shingijutsu, means, and how that meaning informs the production method that Shingijutsu teaches. This is key to understanding Shingijutsu-kaizen correctly.

The Japanese word "shingijutsu" literally means "new technology," as in new *management* technology. "Shin" means "new," and "gijutsu" means "technology." But, this definition does not accurately convey its meaning in the context of Shingijutsu the company.

"Shin" means to make things new. Not to make things new just one time, but to make things new again and again and again. So, not "new," but "new, new, new, new, new…" new forever or always new, continuously new. Therefore, kaizen must be understood as a series of activities pursuing future conditions of what should be in a never-ending cycle of new attempts to improve processes.

The word "gijutsu" has three meanings. The first meaning pertains to Shingijutsu the company, while the second and third meanings do not.

To understand the first meaning of "gijutsu" (技術) we must look carefully at the word "jutsu"(術). This Chinese character consists of inserting 求 in the middle of 行. 求

means demand or request or ask for, and 行 means behave or act or do or practice. This means the practical skills and capabilities to search for abnormalities with the intent to make normal by doing with one's hands. "Jutsu"(術), therefore, requests that action be taken to think by one's hands in genba.

The second meaning of "gijutsu" (技述) means to just talk, speak, discuss, or document what is already known. The character 述 still includes 求, but is not supported by 行 and is therefore different from the first meaning and 求 is just sitting on the 辶. As a result, actions are not taken even if the intent is to pursue abnormalities. Only the first meaning does that.

The third meaning of "gijutsu"(偽述) means to tell a lie or to instruct in the wrong ways. This meaning of "gijutsu" is really troublesome because we often witness people who talk falsely or inaccurately about kaizen.

Shingijutsu teaches people how to correct abnormal conditions and bring them to as close to normal as possible by going to the genba and practicing kaizen.

In summary, the company name, Shingijutsu, means the practical skill to relentlessly search for the root cause of abnormalities by repeatedly asking why and taking concrete actions to prevent recurrences, with the intent to make normal, and do this with one's hands to forever create the new.

This meaning informs the Shingijutsu Production SiQmi. The term "SiQmi" stands for Systematic Integration of

Quality Material and Information. It is a play on the Japanese words for the numbers 4 (shi), 9 (ku), and 3 (mi) – the significance of the number 493 will become clear in a moment. You can think of the term "SiQmi" as having the meaning of "methods" ("hoshiki," in Japanese) or "countermeasures" to abnormalities that exist within a specific context of a business or organization. Therefore, there is a SiQmi for everything. This is the basic way of thinking for all activities.

SiQmi differs from the term "system," which suggests there is one system and therefore only one best way. In fact, there are many, many ways, ways that are evolving over time, hence the term SiQmi.

On one of his birthdays, Nakao-san said:

> "Kaizen is the series of continuous activities to pursue the shapes of what should be. In order to achieve this, many different SiQmi's are necessary which include rules, standards, laws, mechanisms and so forth. They are infinite and we, in Japan, count 50,000 symbolically. Among infinite number of SiQmi, still seven mudas remain unsolved, always, even after many kaizens are thoroughly and exhaustedly practiced. I have never seen the genba with less than 7 muda's yet. I hope the spirit of Shingijutsu Production SiQmi will be succeeded by many people for a long time."

Nakao-san teaches that you must try many different ideas and possibilities to improve, yet, even though you have made improvements, there are many new variations and combinations that remain for you to try.

No matter what people do to correct the abnormal conditions that exist within the specific context of a business or organization, seven types of waste (muda) remain:

- People – Waiting
- Products – Overproduction
- Equipment
- Processes
    - Processing/Machining
    - Inspection/Defects or Correction
    - Transportation
    - Stagnation including Inventory

Therefore, there is no such thing as a "perfect process," just as there is no such thing as the "perfect person." Even the "perfect person" has bad habits. This may be difficult to understand at first. But, it will become clear the more that you develop your practical skills to search for abnormalities and by making improvements with your own hands.

Humanity must be respected in order to achieve these outcomes. People must be allowed to think and participate in the improvement of their own work. It is very important to encourage them to fully use their wisdom coming from their experiences at the genba. Kaizen develops human capabilities and is the process that converts the words "respect for humanity" into reality.

Nakao-san teaches: "The seven wastes are like a disease

that you cannot completely eliminate." He encourages people by saying "try, try, try." He means to think, be creative, and try making improvements with your own hands, by getting your hands dirty. Nakao-san says: "Trystorming is most important. Never stop trying."

2

Shingijutsu-Kaizen

The word "leadership" in Japanese means to guide someone by taking them by their fingers, to persuade by showing how to do something in practice until they understand. This is "learn by doing." This is Shingijutsu-kaizen.

The focal point of *Kaizen Forever* is "genba kaizen." The Japanese word "genba" means "actual place," as in the actual place where work is performed and the places of the targets of kaizen. The Japanese word "kaizen" means "change things to make them better" or "change for the better." Therefore, "genba kaizen" means "change for the better at the actual place where work is performed."

Keep in mind that some changes may possibly make the things worse than before if you make changes before you understand the change. Take the case of layout change. First, clearly define what you want to change, then simulate the change using mock-ups prior to making the actual layout change.

The context of the word "kaizen" is critically important in order to correctly grasp its meaning. First, the genba workers need to receive the benefits of kaizen. Then, kaizen, change for the better, must benefit everyone. If an improvement is made that negatively impacts someone or a process upstream or downstream, then "change for the better" has not occurred. People must not be harmed by kaizen. If they are, then "change for the better" has not occurred. Managers must not fire people as a result of kaizen. The requirement for non-zero-sum (win-win) outcomes is what makes it a challenge to understand and correctly practice kaizen. Please aim to improve the whole and never give up. Then, everybody involved in kaizen will feel a sense of achievement and fulfillment.

Not all kaizen is the same. In fact, there are vast differences. Shingijutsu-kaizen is people-focused training on how to improve processes and achieve flow. When material-and-information flows, many beneficial outcomes that ultimately reduce overall costs are realized such as:

- Higher quality
- Shorter lead-time
- Higher customer satisfaction
- Higher market share
- Higher profits

This is done without harming people. In fact, this can only be done by developing human resources, to conduct and lead kaizen effectively.

Most managers add capital assets to generate cash. In Shingijutsu-kaizen, capital assets are reduced to generate more cash. For example, simpler equipment will achieve the expected results without the need for expensive equipment that people always desire.

As Nakao-san teaches:

"To make good product, you have to make good people. Because good people do not always make good products, kaizen is necessary. In this way, both people and product improve."

Likewise, to make good service, you have to make good people who will become teachers of teachers in series for kaizen forever, developing and improving people's skills and capabilities as the heart of kaizen. It inspires people to do great things.

The structure and process of kaizen has been described elsewhere. Shingijutsu emphasizes the importance of the mindset and spirit of kaizen to create better processes with flow. This is difficult to convey. But, if we are successful, we will achieve our goal of inspiring the younger generation to practice Shingijutsu-kaizen. Shingijutsu-kaizen is humanity-centered training in process improvement. That means, fundamentally, that people are at the center of kaizen and respected. This translates into confidence in their ability to comprehend the existence of abnormalities and improve flow using their own ideas and creativity – especially in the context of teamwork, free of organizational politics and other disrupting influences.

But, kaizen team members' ideas and creativity will be poor if they are permitted to think in the same ways that they have always thought about dealing with abnormalities. Instead, they must be given many strict constraints. Abnormalities are recognized when standards exist. Without standards, abnormalities will not be seen or acted upon which prevents attainment of the normal condition.

Constraints disrupt paradigms related to the approaches taken to correct abnormalities, so that changes made actually result in cost reduction through productivity improvements by various means. Strict constraints challenge people to think and be creative in ways that they have not done before. This is the key to making improvements quickly and at low or no cost that help to achieve flow.

Nakao-san's "Nos"

An extraordinary feature of Shingijutsu-kaizen is Nakao-san's "Nos," which should be understood as strong prohibitions in the sense of "Must Not." Nakao-san's "Nos" are things that people must not do (see "Abnormal vs. Normal Condition" image at the end of Chapter 4).

For example, "no money" means to use the existing materials and additional money must not be spent; "no people" means to eliminate the muda and fully utilize the existing human resources and additional people must not be hired; "no set-up time" means everything should be arranged off the machine beforehand and the set-up changes should be completed in one second; "no three-handed operations" means we must not use legs or mouth for the third hand.

Kaizen team members must make improvements under the following conditions:

- No money
- No people
- No space
- No cranes

- No conveyors
- No set-up time
- No push production
- No warehouse
- No band aids / rework
- No three-handed operations
- No roots
- No vines
- No islands
- No concrete heads
- No drawers
- No cabinet doors
- No lift trucks (for horizontal movement)
- No monuments
- No computers
- No too many parts
- No batches
- No adjustments
- No hammers
- No extra machines
- No piling up
- No catalog engineer
- No shared resources
- No pallets
- No weld assembly jigs
- No final assembly jigs
- No "M" machines
- No status quo
- No sacred cows

These are just some of Nakao-san's "Nos." There can be

more depending on the process that is being improved. Nakao-san's "Nos" provide an effective framework for generating ideas, stimulating creativity, and eliminating obstacles that disturb flow.

Initially, some kaizen team members think Nakao-san's "Nos" are crazy and that they limit their ability to improve, and so they resist his directives. After a day or two of kaizen, they comply with his direction and begin to realize that the emerging outcome reveals many more and bigger abnormalities than they initially thought. What seemed impossible at first is now within reach.

Nakao-san's "Nos" release kaizen team members from shackles that have bound them to traditional ways of thinking about and dealing with abnormalities. This is liberating. It frees the mind to become a brave explorer, never again to be satisfied being a timid conformist.

This gives you a sense of the power of Shingijutsu-kaizen. It is dynamic, inspiring, exciting, fun, and invigorating. Team members go into Shingijutsu-kaizen skeptical and come out happy, proud, and amazed. Here are some typical remarks made by team members:

"I would have never believed that could be done if I did not see it with my own eyes."

"I know now I know nothing!"

"I was assigned to this kaizen team. I didn't think much of it. I am amazed by what I learned."

"I finally see hope."

For most people, Shingijutsu-kaizen is a life-changing experience. That is not the case with common kaizen, called "kairyo" in Japanese, meaning simply "to change things." Shingijutsu-kaizen is the result of the lineage of kaizen passed from Mr. Ohno who trained and disciplined Nakao-san, and its evolution post-1987.

Remember, we engage in kaizen for the purpose of reducing costs and improving productivity by changing processes from batch-and-queue (stagnation) to flow.

Please think about this:

- How do Nakao-san's "Nos" develop people's capabilities?
- Can you deduce how each "No" helps improve material-and-information flow?
- Each "No" plays a specific role in helping to make material-and-information flow. What role do they play?
- Can you see beyond the surface to comprehend the details of how each "No" helps improve flow, and its relationship to the people who perform the process?
- What are the financial and economic impacts of each "No?"
- What are the "No" analogues for improving processes in a hospital, a university, a retailer, or a government agency? Are they not the same? How so?

Moonshine

Nakao-san's "Nos," his "Must Nots," set the stage for "Moonshine," another part of Shingijutsu-kaizen. Nakao-san has been called Moonshine-sensei for some time. Shingijutsu Company decided to call him "Father of Moonshine" (F.O.M.) internally as well as externally, as his official title since 2005. Why is Nakao-san called the Father of Moonshine? He is called the Father of Moonshine for the unique way in which he has promoted (and insisted on) the use of low-cost solutions to correct abnormalities.

History has shown that many important inventions and discoveries were made in the hidden corners of an organization or were sometimes driven by unusual thinking or behaviors. We usually need some new and specific tools or devices on these occasions to help make innovations at the genba and quickly confirm the effects of changes.

Kaizen activities are the tool or method that helps people make inventions and discoveries. Kaizen takes place in whatever the existing condition happens to be with respect to money, space, and people. Meaning, no money should be spent, no space should be added, no new people should be hired. It is within this framework that people must try to devise a continuous stream of innovative new solutions to abnormalities.

Nakao-san has always emphasized the importance of making inventions and discoveries within existing conditions while he taught kaizen. Then one day, an American participating in kaizen said: "This is moonshine." The comment referred to the U.S. Prohibition law that strictly controlled liquor production and which quickly led to widespread illegal production of liquor called "moonshine."

Today, large banners saying "Moonshine" hang in the factories of some companies to encourage kaizen. Recently, Nakao-san has helped a liquor company in Japan regain its profitability and competitiveness, and it has produced a liquor for sale under the label "Moonshine" in honor of sensei Nakao.

Nakao-san defines moonshine as:

> "Developing valuable solutions to abnormalities by creatively adapting materials that are already on hand. It requires looking at those materials and the abnormalities themselves with a renewed perspective of doing a lot with a little."

Therefore, moonshine challenges people to make improvements with surplus, re-worked, or re-purposed materials. In contrast, people confronted with a abnormality are quick to buy expensive things to fix abnormalities. Even small businesses have excess materials laying around that can be used to improve processes. There is no need to spend money. Use your brain instead.

Improving processes must result in cost reduction through productivity improvement by various means. Reducing costs means using ideas and creativity instead of spending money. Reducing costs means improving quality. Reducing costs means reducing lead-times. Reducing costs means material-and-information must flow. Continuously reduce costs by eliminating abnormal conditions to get closer to the standard.

An important aspect of Moonshine is to think about how nature solves abnormalities. How does nature design solutions to abnormalities? What materials does nature use? What is the structure of the solutions? How to they communicate and integrate with their surroundings? How do nature's solutions evolve over time and adapt to changing circumstances?

Moonshine adds a fun element to kaizen and strengthens teamwork. It challenges people make many prototypes, trials, and simulations in a few hours or a few days, compared to the normal timescale for improvements of months or years. It encourages people to develop a habit of quickly creating prototypes and conducting simulations as a fun activity – a hobby. This is called "shumilation," which is a combination of the Japanese word for hobby, "shumi," and the word "simulation." Shumilation makes kaizen more fun.

As Nakao-san teaches:

"Quick and dirty is better than slow and elaborate."

This is a nice saying, but why is it so? Do not blindly accept words without understanding their meaning deeply.

- What does "quick and dirty" do that slow and fancy cannot?

- How does it affect employees, suppliers, customer, investors, and communities?
- What are the social and economic impacts of "quick and dirty?"

The purpose of Shingijutsu-kaizen is to improve processes, from batch-and-queue (stagnation) to flow, and to create a new way of thinking about processes. It is to create ingenious ways to work simpler, with better communication, teamwork, quality, and in less time (which must never be equated to working faster or speeding people up).

There is a beginning and an end to each Shingijutsu-kaizen. Positive results have been obtained. But, what have people learned from that experience? Firstly, they learn that they must apply what they learned in Shingijutsu-kaizen to daily process improvement. New, new, new... new forever, always new, continuously new. Do not forget Nakao-san's "Nos." Keep using them. Do not forget about Moonshine. Keep doing that.

Too many people think they know the basics when they do not. Stick to the basics. Focus on flow. Master the basics, and then improve from there.

The philosophy of Shingijutsu-kaizen is the basic way of thinking that one must possess to practice kaizen correctly. And, this basic way of thinking is not static, but develops and improves over time to improve people's kaizen experience and kaizen results.

PRACTICAL EXERCISE

What "Must Nots" are part of your kaizens,
or must become part of your kaizens?
The more "Must Nots," the better.

Moonshine Liquor

Photo by Katsusaburo Yoshino

Red label (left) and the more expensive
Black label liquor (right) with their packages.

Guidance on Nakao-san's Teachings

Chapters 3 through 9 contain a selection of Nakao-san's many teachings on People, Process, Equipment, Space, Money, Time, and Information.

We present his teachings as separate chapters to reduce confusion. However, Nakao-san does not teach that way. And, we do not comprehend his teachings that way.

Nakao-san teaches about People, Process, Equipment, Space, Money, Time, and Information in combination with one another. This reveals the interconnections between them and enlightens and deepens our awareness of cost reduction through productivity improvement by various means and the creation of good flow.

Do not comprehend Nakao-san's teachings separately. Please think about the interconnections between the teachings in Chapters 3 through Chapter 9. It is very important that you do this.

3

Teachings on People

Ask yourself many questions for each of these teachings, such as: Why is it necessary? What abnormalities can be rectified and made closer to the standard? How does it improve flow? How does it help people? How does it improve the business? Have new abnormalities been created? What have I learned? What improvement comes next? And so on.

Nakao-san taught us this, and more, about people:

Be respectful of others. Respect humanity. People are central.

Respect operators by eliminating their burdens.

Failure is not failure. It is a step towards improvement.

Kaizen should come from operators' complaints.

Put the facts in management's face.

Kaizen should result in Ah-Ha! moments. This gets people to kindergarten level.

Don't do exactly as I say or did not say. Think for yourself.

You have to struggle to squeeze your intelligence out.

It's OK to fail. You're allowed to fail.

Kaizen is not for cutting jobs. Use wisdom and ingenuity to protect people's lives.

I am strict on people. I used to 'fire' everyone; now only once in a while when someone tells me the reasons why they cannot do it.

An owner or manager who cannot identify 100 things to improve before lunch should not be allowed to eat lunch. They need to be able to point out a new improvement in 10 seconds.

You have to go back to zero. Put yourself under dire circumstances to think differently.

Build your capabilities in-house. Do not rely on outsiders.

Listening and understanding is not enough. You have to practice it. It has to become your skill, your philosophy, and your knowledge. That is how you evolve and develop your own path.

Brainstorming is nothing but thinking in the head. Trystorming is thinking with your hands.

Use your hands to think and feet to see. Make your hands dirty.

Be brave and try it out.

Learn from nature, the treasure of mechanism created over millions of years.

It's OK. He needs to struggle a little bit.

He makes no excuse so I have no reason to scold him.

I want to praise him. But, as soon as I praise him it stops his growth.

Training is a must do. Don't forget training.

I want you to think about this.

Apply the 30-40-30 rule. Direct 40 percent of the people who will listen to join 30 percent of the people who are eager to learn, and do not be bothered by the other 30 percent of people who sometimes view the benefits of kaizen negatively or are skeptical and do not participate in kaizen activities.

Can't think of ideas? Hit the center of your forehead with your closed left hand. Ideas will flow out.

You don't need what you think you need.

The important thing is to extract wisdom from people. That is why I scold them, raise my voice, and praise them. This gets them to 10 years of age level.

Convert the culture from complex to simple.

You do not need the engineers who want to have robots and machining centers.

People make products; therefore, you must develop people.

Why? Why? Always express abnormalities in terms of: When, by whom, where, with what, in what way, how. 5W and 1H.

Generate intelligence instead of generating waste.

All departments should be helping the genba. Only genba is where profit is made.

Make visible what you cannot see. Learn, review, have a deep conversation, compete, engage in friendly battles of words (debates) like Tom and Jerry.

The production line is alive. Develop people to develop the production line.

Executives must not make light of operators. They must discipline themselves to wipe operators' shoes.

Everyone should think about how to create value and make profit.

Think by doing. Don't start thinking before doing.

Action creates wisdom.

Come up with 7 ways to do that.

Master the basics.

Managers have to show people how to do the task. Don't tell.

You will succeed. Be confident!

Pass what you have learned to the next generation.

PRACTICAL EXERCISE

Which teachings on People do you need to better comprehend and emphasize in your practice of kaizen? Why?

How People React to Kaizen

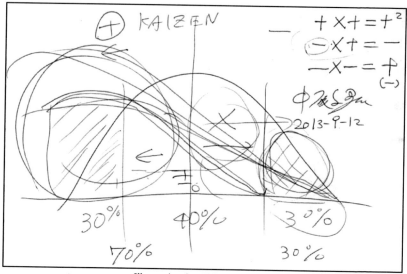

Illustration by Chihiro Nakao. Courtesy of Whitcraft Group

Nakao-san explains how people react to kaizen using the 30-40-30 rule. 30 percent will not learn kaizen (right), 40 percent will listen (middle), and 30 percent are eager to learn kaizen (left). Work to move the middle 40 percent to the left. Then you have 70 percent who will learn kaizen and quickly move the company forward. The last 30 percent who do not look excited about kaizen today will surely be impressed positively by the 70 percent of people and will become interested in kaizen soon.

4

Teachings on Process

Ask yourself many questions for each of these teachings, such as: Why is it necessary? What abnormalities can be rectified and made closer to the standard? How does it improve flow? How does it help people? How does it improve the business? Have new abnormalities been created? What have I learned? What improvement comes next? And so on.

Nakao-san taught us this, and more, about process:

Standard work shows what is actually going on. Standard work is the truth.

No abnormality is an abnormality.

Can the operator be proud of doing this process in front of their spouse or kids? Respect people. Don't waste operator's life.

This is not to make work harder. It is to make work simpler.

The real place, real thing. Always confirm the truth at the actual place with the actual things.

The genba equals reality. The truth lies only at the genba.

If one does not visit the genba, one cannot describe it with drawings or experience the five senses.

The process cannot be understood if language describing the process is imprecise.

Build a process first, then equipment comes.

Make the process jiko kanketsu (self-contained; all resources necessary for flow are contained within the cell).

Material and information must flow together.

The worst state is the current state.

You must work hard to build a process that finds the defect and does not pass it on.

Break complicated processes into small parts.

Material-and-information that goes on journeys suffers quality abnormalities.

Separate the normal situation from abnormal situation.

Shut down production immediately when abnormalities are detected.

Think of the individual functions that need to be performed one piece at a time.

You just have to brush your teeth. Do you have to take off all your clothes to do that?

Processes should be people-centered with simple house-made equipment as needed.

Big machines make it hard to break processes down.

Visualize the mountain (the entire factory), examine the forest (line), look at the trees (process) simultaneously.

Process one piece at a time. That is the principle.

Your mouth is the start of the process. Think of your stomach when you do the work. You take one bite at a time and send it to your stomach.

Do you eat more when you are full? Where will the food go if we eat more when we are full?

When you go to the restroom, don't you flush every time?

Think about washing dentures, then you will think of something. Imagine a toothbrush and create a flow that way.

Take the same approach as mother sets up the kitchen.

You wash your face every morning. You don't wait 10 days to wash your face.

Think of your stack of paper as people. The bottom person will be stressed and will have difficulty breathing. A stack of two means turn on the andon light.

Break down the process. Define the steps. Break it down into 10-second intervals to separate the functions.

Think of the ways that even one person can do it.

Separate the process into its details: man, machine, materials.

Connect the flow. Never disconnect.

Parts that travel all over the place don't have parents or a home.

If production lines are physically moving, then you can see what is going on.

Think about the way a rice farmer tends a rice paddy.

In baseball, the manager is on the genba during the game, not after the game. It's too late then.

Aren't you reporting the results in genba yesterday at today's morning meeting? It's too late. We already lost half a day.

Why don't you think to improve it 10 times as much?

Lift or move things with one finger.

You have to do 100 percent quality check/inspection. Use go/no-go gages for quick check.

Inspection is waste, but we need to do it for quality assurance. Do it in one second.

What did you have for dinner 10 days ago? Everybody remembers what they ate a few hours ago. With batch, you keep making defects but don't know how or when you made the defect.

Statistical sampling forces batching. Think of 100 inspect/check without additional processing.

Today's jobs need today's tooling. Get rid of tooling for tomorrow's job. Tomorrow's tooling is early enough tomorrow.

Inventories don't give you peace of mind. They give you abnormalities. Inventories are expenses to keep someone's mind safe, not keeping the company safe.

Batch is stagnant, stop-and-go production. That's no good.

Outsourcing leads to batch-processing.

Do you wipe someone else's butt? You should not pay for someone else's failure. Ask: Why are we doing this ridiculous thing?

What is the purpose of being born and being here if you do re-work or fix people's mistakes?

With flow, you realize a mistake right away and you can correct it right away.

Things have to be moving. That is normal.

For every process, the subsequent process is the customer. You must make the finest quality item in the unit of one.

Stagnation is the invisible unnecessary inventory. This is the worst.

Production lines must evolve to improve ergonomics so that people come to work and get healthy, get fit.

Daily exercise and daily training is similar to chaku-chaku line.

PRACTICAL EXERCISE

Which teachings on Process do you need to better comprehend and emphasize in your practice of kaizen? Why?

Abnormal vs. Normal Condition

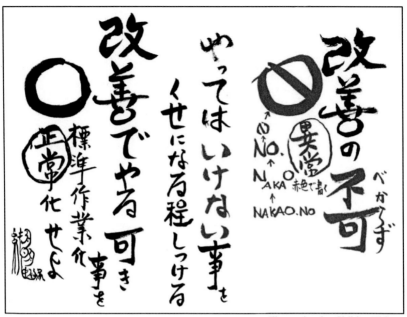

Illustration by Chihiro Nakao

Nakao-san explains normal condition must be established to recognize abnormal condition. From right to left: Kaizen "Must Nots." The name "Nakao" is deconstructed from the international symbol for "no" to read "red no" ("aka" means "red" in Japanese; abnormal conditions must be written in red). Have discipline for the dos and must not dos (red characters) until they become habit. Make the must dos standard work and normalize (open circle). Symbol for "Moonshine" and Nakao Chihiro signature (lower left).

5

Teachings on Equipment

Ask yourself many questions for each of these teachings, such as: Why is it necessary? What abnormalities can be rectified and made closer to the standard? How does it improve flow? How does it help people? How does it improve the business? Have new abnormalities been created? What have I learned? What improvement comes next? And so on.

Nakao-san taught us this, and more, about equipment:

Engineers get tricked by machine manufacturers.

Processes should not be equipment-centered. Machines must not be considered prior to the process design.

You don't need big, expensive equipment that has wide-ranging capabilities.

If you buy a machine, buy the functions of a machine only. Buy "naked" machines.

Machines must be right-sized and point-of-use.

Machines should be shoulder-wide.

Everyone has similar machines. It is how you use the machine that makes the difference.

Computers kill your ability to think.

Coordinate measuring machine is OK for measuring gages, but not product.

Value in a machine is to do a specific operation on a specific part at a specific company.

One process, one machine.

You have to identify the professional way to use the machine.

Build equipment that suits the process you design.

Make simplified equipment that matches your takt time.

Build something so you can have some fun.

If you build a small machine on your own, you can fix it yourself.

Layout must enable process flow.

Measurement does not tell you if something is good or bad. Quickly check and use go/no-go gages instead.

Machines should be quiet. Operators should not wear earplugs.

Throw out the tools and jigs just bought from outside. Produce self-made tools and jigs that fit the products to manufacture instead.

I am surprised you are paying engineers to make heavy, complex, expensive, tooling. It is kindergarten, not professional.

Never buy nor build a tool or jig that turns into junk.

When you break and divide the process down, you can create simple, low-cost fixtures.

Make fixtures that fit the environment of time and era.

Buying big machines during growth periods generates costs in downturns. People forget about downturns.

Develop engineers by making equipment in-house vs. buying from outside.

You don't need to purchase complicated gages. Make simple gages yourself.

Indicator gages are no good because they must be interpreted. Use go/no-go gages.

Fork lift function is vertical lifting, not horizontal material transportation.

Continue Moonshine forever, then you will succeed.

PRACTICAL EXERCISE

Which teachings on Equipment do you need to better comprehend and emphasize in your practice of kaizen? Why?

Equipment That Improves Flow

Photo by Bob Emiliani

A genba operator building a right-sized hot forming press by himself using existing materials. The press meets the takt time and produces just the necessary quantity. The small part was produced on a large press requiring 400 square feet of space. The right-sized hot forming press requires only 18 square feet. The right-sized press fits into the flowline thereby reducing part travel by a large distance. Operator ergonomics and safety are improved, while energy consumption and process cycle times are also greatly reduced.

6

Teachings on Space

Ask yourself many questions for each of these teachings, such as: Why is it necessary? What abnormalities can be rectified and made closer to the standard? How does it improve flow? How does it help people? How does it improve the business? Have new abnormalities been created? What have I learned? What improvement comes next? And so on.

Nakao-san taught us this, and more, about space:

Throw this out! Get rid of this!

Take down the shelves.

Close the warehouse!

Distribution centers are stagnation centers.

Disconnecting manufacturing from the marketplace slows down or impairs automatic reflexes.

Don't hide embarrassing objects. Make them visible so these mistakes are never made again.

Warehouses hold unnecessary things that you pay taxes on for years.

Offices and cubicles are like jail cells. What did people do wrong to get treated like that?

Convert warehouses and inventory into small stores at the genba.

Break down physical barriers between people so that they can work together.

Put small parts in small containers.

Eliminate preconceived notions.

Stand on the shop floor and see reality.

Make everything obeya. It also costs less.

You must be able to see the whole picture and the details at the same time: The mountain, the forest, and the trees.

Normal common sense says fill the warehouse. I say throw everything out and keep only what is truly needed for today and tomorrow.

Right-size equipment to reduce space and connect processes.

Machines and equipment should not be greater than body-width.

Why is there a cage here? These people did nothing wrong. Don't put people behind cages.

How many people take a bath at one time? Wash one piece at a time in a small container.

Practice at the genba rather than criticize.

PRACTICAL EXERCISE

Which teachings on Space do you need to better
comprehend and emphasize in your practice of kaizen?
Why?

Close the Warehouse

Photo by Bob Emiliani

Nakao-san writes: "Empty this by 2014.12.25." They emptied the warehouse and then totally shut it down.

7

Teachings on Money

Ask yourself many questions for each of these teachings, such as:
Why is it necessary? What abnormalities can be rectified and made
closer to the standard? How does it improve flow? How does it help
people? How does it improve the business? Have new abnormalities
been created? What have I learned? What improvement
comes next? And so on.

Nakao-san taught us this, and more, about money:

> In order to change better, use some wisdom but not money.

> It feels good to spend money. Stop it!

> Owners' financial vision far exceeds their actual financial condition.

> Genba is what's important. Only genba generates profit.

> You have to transform the business so it gets profits.

> Value of the shop floor is if you are making something you can sell.

> Flow is lowest operating cost and lowest fixed asset base to pay taxes on.

> Bankers and investors want to spend money first. They

believe money makes money. Owners should not do that. They should make improvement first and then judge if monetary expenditure is truly necessary.

You receive wages because you are professionals. To get paid as professional, you have to apply intelligence to make things better.

You are paid for yesterday. Professionals must think about making things better tomorrow.

Professionals have to offer equal value of performance to pay.

Activities that you have to do but add no value must be simplified because they do not make any money.

Do it using existing resources.

Buying expensive machines is like 30 years of bad relationships. This is not desirable.

The more equipment you install, the less profit you make.

Once you purchase equipment, you have to pay taxes on it. It sucks profits out of the business.

You have to pay depreciation and taxes on durable jigs and tooling. No good. Use simple clamps instead.

Don't buy things you have to pay taxes on. Make it yourself.

Throw away expensive tools and jigs you purchased when the job is done. Don't spend money for muda. This is the largest lesson to prevent re-occurrence.

Design processes for low taxes.

Old tools and jigs are a tax bonanza for government.

Use old tools and jigs for museum for training purposes.

Is it truly necessary to spend money on new equipment or hire more people? Go to the genba to know.

Use Creform® and build what you need.

Do quick check after every operation. That is how you build in quality.

In order to get profit, first make the hidden things come to the surface and visible and then reduce the time, space, machines, materials, and people – never through layoffs.

PRACTICAL EXERCISE

Which teachings on Money do you need to better
comprehend and emphasize in your practice of kaizen?
Why?

Cost Knowledge vs. Cost Awareness

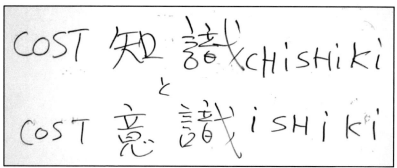

Illustration by Chihiro Nakao

Nakao-san writes these words on a white board to teach the difference between cost knowledge ("chishiki") and cost awareness ("ishiki"). University study and MBA degrees teach cost as knowledge. Only the genba teaches the spirit and awareness of cost reduction.

8

Teachings on Time

*Ask yourself many questions for each of these teachings, such as:
Why is it necessary? What abnormalities can be rectified and made
closer to the standard? How does it improve flow? How does it help
people? How does it improve the business? Have new abnormalities
been created? What have I learned? What improvement
comes next? And so on.*

Nakao-san taught us this, and more, about time:

> Hold your breath to measure time. If you get light-headed it is taking too long.

> What if the company had only one person? Because you have many people, you have made the process complex and time-consuming. Excessive division of labor ends up with inefficiency.

> One touch, one second.

> Measure time with a stopwatch, in seconds.

> Make the change-over equal to the time you can hold your breath.

> Just because the customer gives you a lot of time does not mean you should take it.

> Managers must challenge themselves and strive for production that surpasses the current state using

lightning speed, courage, and determination.

Queue time is stagnation. Make work flow smoothly and quickly.

From when to when: What time will you start, what time will you finish? Always be conscious of time.

Try things quickly.

When "in-time" is over-emphasized, everything is done far ahead of time. Always be sure to be Just-in-Time! Just-on-time sounds good but is not practical. Just-in time is the best.

Take pride in your work to match cycle times as a physician takes pride in their work to cure people.

Move upstairs work (e.g. programming, inspection methods, engineering) downstairs to the genba.

The process is normal when it flows.

Equipment-based improvement takes time and costs money.

The standard is the least amount of time consumed. Kaizen from there.

Professionals should not take more than 16 seconds to do a job.

Make it and sell it immediately, like a sushi bar.

Computer measuring machines create bottlenecks. Do manual one second check with go/no-go gages.

Not enough people eat fish eyes. That is why there are so many concrete heads.

One breath, one minute, one second. Place a high value on "1."

Do you take bread out of the toaster to measure its temperature and put it back in? You don't do such a stupid thing. Measure the part in the machine.

Do not call them "suppliers." Call them "partners," which implies equals.

Engineers working in the office create a big expensive fixture and spend months doing it. Engineers should make tools with their hands, not with their heads.

Common sense makes things difficult. Therefore, things take much longer than is necessary and cost a lot more. Do the opposite: make things simple.

People will start calling you crazy. You are not crazy. Sacred cow people are crazy. Don't blame them. It's the environment. Now you understand why you must make changes. Create a new environment.

Do you know if you are you on-time? Behind time? Ahead of time? Standard? Abnormal?

Always have the intention to do kaizen.

You're still thinking in your head. You need to use your hands.

To try is the same as 100 times thinking.
Consider inventory like fish; it goes bad over time.

I want you to cut a digit from that number (360 seconds). Do it in 36 seconds.

Load-unload while holding your breath. Then you will think of better ways.

Managers must be humble, otherwise the team members will not follow. Team members will not come up with good ideas. Team members will not produce good results.

PRACTICAL EXERCISE

Which teachings on Time do you need to better comprehend and emphasize in your practice of kaizen? Why?

How to Make Improvements Quickly

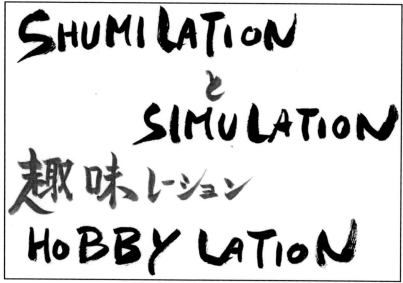

Illustration by Chihiro Nakao

Nakao-san teaches how to make kaizen fun. Moonshine involves making many prototypes and doing many simulations. "Shumi" in Japanese means "hobby." Shumilation means to make kaizen with Moonshine a fun hobby so that people will do it every day and even all night if necessary.

9

Teachings on Information

Ask yourself many questions for each of these teachings, such as: Why is it necessary? What abnormalities can be rectified and made closer to the standard? How does it improve flow? How does it help people? How does it improve the business? Have new abnormalities been created? What have I learned? What improvement comes next? And so on.

Nakao-san taught us this, and more, about information:

University teaches cost as a knowledge. But the genba teaches the awareness for cost reduction.

Trying things is the best.

When you physically do it, your hands will think for you.

If you were just thinking in your head, you would not know about these abnormalities. That's why you must think with your hands.

Managers must stand on the shop floor and observe.

One cannot understand the true facts from an office desk or report. Inconvenient information will never surface.

The genba reveals the subjects that the engineers must correct in their design.

Kaizen eyes see 1000 things needing improvement.

People are too smart. They think with their head always. This causes stress and worry. This causes you to drink.

Don't just force team members to make visual controls for their use. They are for your use as a manager.

Engineers must go to the genba.

Capture information in sketches. Don't use words.

Verify first article in quality clinic. Do not bring epidemic of defects – batches of dead parts – to quality clinic.

People give too much information all at once.

Give only information that is needed when it is needed in the amount needed.

Standard work is a communication tool for managers and workers.

Data comes to managers. That is incorrect. Managers must go to the data (shop floor).

Managers must manage by seeing the genba, not by reading.

No brainstorming; do trystorming.

Maintain conditions that prevent abnormalities from recurring using andons.

Working quickly with your hands gets a faster result than thinking with the computer.

Put lipstick on once.

Managers must practice 5 Whys rather than criticize.

Even if you don't think it will work, try it anyway.

More wisdom will surely come out once we lack in workforce, materials, equipment, and money than the circumstances satisfied with having resources in excess.

The worst manager is one who looks only at reports.

The customer is not willing to pay for information beyond which is necessary but to pay for what they need.

PRACTICAL EXERCISE

Which teachings on Information do you need to better comprehend and emphasize in your practice of kaizen? Why?

Guidance on Nakao-san's Teachings

We again remind you that Nakao-san's teachings on People, Process, Equipment, Space, Money, Time, and Information related to the products and services produced are given in combination, not separately, as we have presented.

Please think about the interconnections between the teachings in Chapters 3 through 9. It is very important that you do this.

Finally, please do not memorize and blindly repeat Nakao-san's teachings. Doing so will result in kaizen malpractice.

The purpose of this book is to teach younger generations, to inspire them to learn and practice kaizen and achieve flow. Also, this book encourages you to think for yourself and go to the genba. Unless you go to the genba, the learning about kaizen will never be yours.

Office Material-and-Information Flow

Photo by Bob Emiliani

Creating flowlines in the office enhances awareness for cost reduction through a reduction in lead-time and improved quality, and improves cooperation, and teamwork for kaizen.

10
Shingijutsu-Kaizen Process

Shingijutsu-kaizen is people-focused kaizen based on "learn by doing." It is a humanistic approach to kaizen that helps people realize their full potential. Shingijutsu-kaizen helps people develop confidence in themselves, their wisdom, and their capability to improve. It pushes people to think differently and to not be afraid of making changes.

Common sense makes work difficult, time-consuming, and expensive. Shingijutsu-kaizen teaches the opposite of that. The focus is on simplification, doing the work in only the time it actually takes to do the work, not spending money, and to do work in ways that lower costs and produce many other favorable outcomes.

Nakao-san typically facilitates five kaizen teams at one time. Four teams in the shop and one in the office, for example. All kaizens are held at the genba. There is no "classroom kaizen" or "conference room kaizen." Shingijutsu-kaizen focuses kaizen team members on flow and making work easier, not on targets such as xx percent, because good numbers will follow as a result of flow. This is an important lesson.

Analysis of operators' work, whether in the shop or office, is performed with the aid of a stopwatch and these one-page forms:

- Takt time calculation
- Standardized production capacity sheet
- Time observation form
- Yamazumi chart (cycle time)
- Standard work sheet
- Standard work combination sheet
- Target and result sheet
- Kaizen newspaper

This is how productivity is improved, costs reduced, and quality is assured. You must master the basics. The general process is as follows:

First Day

- Kaizen teams present their subjects to deal with to Nakao-san.
- Nakao-san provides direction for improvement.
- Kaizen teams go to the genba and get to know the facts there.
- Nakao-san visits each team twice in the morning to learn what they have done and provide more direction.
- Nakao-san visits each team twice in the afternoon to learn what they have done and provide more direction.
- Before closing the day, team leaders' meetings are held and Nakao-san gives basic direction to each team leader about their activities for the upcoming days.
- Kaizen teams continue working for a while longer.

Second Day and Onward

- Kaizen teams go to the genba and make improvements.
- Nakao-san visits each team twice in the morning to learn what they have done and provide direction.
- Nakao-san visits each team twice in the afternoon to learn what they have done and provide more direction.
- Before closing the day, team leaders' meetings are held and Nakao-san gives basic direction to each team leader about their activities for the upcoming days.
- Kaizen teams continue working for a while longer.

Last Day

- Kaizen teams go to the genba and make improvements, and prepare for the kaizen close-out meeting.
- Each kaizen team presents the results of their work, highlighting improvements made and the direction of future improvements.
- Nakao-san gives encouragement and provides direction on future daily improvement.

Throughout kaizen, Nakao-san demonstrates concepts with found items such as: take-out food container, tape measurer, stapler, toaster oven, chair, coffee cup, door, shirt, water bottle, shoes, paper plate, pen and cap, table, digital camera battery, chopsticks, and notebook, and makes analogies to things such as surgery, the Panama Canal, nature, the home etc.

There is a great deal of physical demonstration as well as a lot of sketching to convey ideas and concepts to kaizen team members. The emphasis is on simplification, making work easier, and flow.

There is also constant eye contact and touching of hands and arms to assure attentiveness and to demonstrate things. Doing this develops heart-to-heart communication and creates heart-to-heart ties between the kaizen consultant and kaizen team members. Another important practice is for each team leader to walk through the genba they are assigned to for kaizen, together with top management, and confirm the facts there.

This reflects how each Shingijutsu consultant has been personally trained by Nakao-san in Shingijutsu-kaizen art and practices.

Kaizen is a fun process that develops human capability in response to competitive business challenges. What do people say at about Shingijutsu-kaizen? Here are some typical remarks made by team members:

"This is the fun part of my job."
"I want to do this every day."
"I can't believe we got paid for doing this."
"This is pretty amazing stuff."
"I'm floored by what we accomplished!"

Comments such as these signal current and future kaizen success.

PRACTICAL EXERCISE

The better prepared you are, the more you will get. What are you going to prepare for the next kaizen?

Nakao Compass

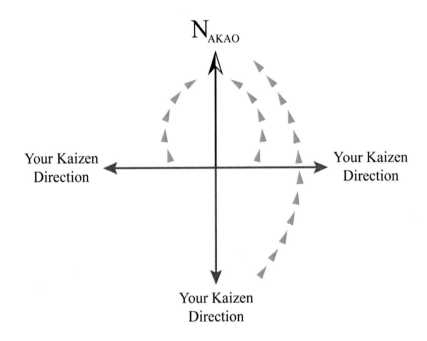

Graphic by Chihiro Nakao

"I have to scold† people to get them to move in my direction."

---

† The Japanese word for "scold" is "shikaru." Nakao-san's scoldings are given to people who make excuses. Scoldings are always followed by helpful guidance towards the "N" (Nakao) direction, to correct or train to become better without negative feelings; training with heart or love, like a parent-child relationship. For example, Nakao-san corrects the method, way of thinking, and speed.

11

Closing Comments

The preceding pages are our attempt to present the soul of kaizen to the next generation. We hope we have been successful at inspiring you to embrace kaizen and set a goal to become a capable practitioner of Shingijutsu-kaizen. Please put into practice what you have learned in this book.

Kaizen is infinite. This small book provides you with enough information to practice kaizen forever, based on current circumstances, the need for that moment, and the time in that era. Reading is good, but you can only learn by doing.

You also have a good understanding of the difference between Shingijutsu-kaizen and common kaizen. But, that is only the beginning. Shingijutsu-kaizen is difficult to copy because it is difficult to understand. It embodies knowledge formed as a result of daily practice. This is critical for the development of an accurate understanding of Shingijutsu-kaizen.

Shingijutsu-kaizen is a way to grow people and grow business. Its participants must always respect humanity and never spoil each individual's personality and grace, whether they are employees, suppliers, customers, investors, or communities.

There is no magic in Shingijutsu-kaizen. The difficult part is to remain committed to kaizen after some improvements have been made. People lose focus after several years. The number of new ideas for improvement decreases and the benefits of kaizen look minimal. This is simply because of the lack of genba visits. Go to the genba and please read this book again to make sure this does not happen. Kaizen must continue and evolve. Be spiritually committed to the long-term continuous journey.

Top management must be committed. But, it is better if top management learns Shingijutsu-kaizen by participating in it. Nakao-san's teachings are relevant to the CEO, president, and every vice president in the company: human resources, operations, information technology, engineering, research and development, sales, marketing, facilities, purchasing, customer service, and finance.

Too often, finance people are missing from kaizen. They do not understand waste and think kaizen is playtime. Everything Nakao-san teaches has financial impact, whether it pertains to cost accounting or classical economics. Flow reverses much of what people are taught about accounting and economics in school, and other subjects as well. Be brave and learn new things.

As the digital age rapidly advances, people ask, "Will kaizen be necessary?" Kaizen will not go away in the digital age. In fact, kaizen will become more important and necessary tomorrow than today. Why? Because machines are inflexible, cannot identify what needs to be improved, lack ideas and creativity, and are slow to respond to changing circumstances. Machines will never do kaizen; only people can do kaizen.

Humans possess unique capabilities that make them the only vessel that can bring kaizen to life.

As Nakao-san teaches:

> "You must do lots of trial-and-error. Don't consider error as failure. Never give up."

A Final Thought

If you understand what you have read in this book, then you do not understand.

Now, let's go to genba!

———————

Nakao-san's drawing of a standing man stresses the importance to going to genba and thinking by using hands and looking by using feet.

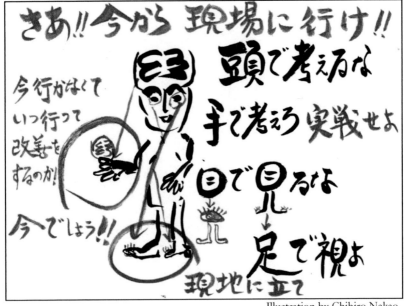

Illustration by Chihiro Nakao

It reads: (right side) Don't think by head but by hands! Just do! Don't look by eyes but by feet! Standing at genchi (actual place) (left side). Unless you go to genba now, when will you go? It is the time now!

Appendix

Kaizen at Home

Nakao-san teaches:

Kaizen is for the workplace only. You must never do kaizen at home. You should relax.

I encourage you to do a lot of wasteful things at home. There is lots of waste in private life and in love. That is OK.

It is not worth being human if we don't think of new things when we are at work. It is OK not to think at home because you are not getting paid by the company. When you are paid by the company, you must work for the company.

Do kaizen at work because waste costs money. In your house, all seven wastes are OK. Your house is not paying you. Ask "Why?" at work, but not at home.

If it is your hobby or private life, there are some good things in waste. But not on the genba at work.

If this is unclear to you, then think what is home for. What is the purpose of home? Think of 50 things.

Acknowledgments

The authors would like express their sincere thanks to Mr. Chihiro Nakao, Ms. Midori Suzuki, Ms. Kanae Hatta, Mr. Tomoyuki Fujii, and Mr. Takahiro Kambe of Shingijutsu USA, and to Jacqueline Gallo, Kate Lynch, Steve Ruggiero, and Jeff Paul of Whitcraft Group, Eastford, Connecticut.

Notes

Please use the following Note pages to reflect on what you have learned from reading *Kaizen Forever*, as well as specific actions that you intend to take. We hope you will do so with the following perspective as taught to us by Nakao-san:

The top of the following Note pages contain the "∞" symbol which means infinite sources of wisdom, teaching or learning.

The infinity symbol is followed by the "," symbol, which means the great number of possibilities or breakthroughs that exist (e.g. comma used every three digits when writing numbers).

∞   Your Infinite Possibilities   ,

∞   Your Infinite Possibilities   ,

∞ Your Infinite Possibilities ,

About the Authors

Bob Emiliani
Dr. Emiliani is a former manager in the aerospace industry and currently a professor at a university in Connecticut.

Katsusaburo Yoshino
Mr. Yoshino is a former manager in the automotive industry, former lecturer at a university in Japan teaching English for engineers, and currently a kaizen consultant with Shingijutsu USA.

Rudy Go
Mr. Go is a former kaizen leader in the aerospace industry and currently a kaizen consultant with Shingijutsu USA.

Disclosure: Bob Emiliani had no contract or business relationship with Shingijutsu USA at the time this book was written.

Made in the USA
San Bernardino, CA
21 September 2017